Kevin Byrne,
Port Laoise,
Co.Laois

Joe Sellars, York

Becky Riches,
Bristol

Susan Millar,
Glasgow

£6.75

A IS FOR ATTILA, THAT NASTY, OLD HUN.

B IS FOR BETCHA I'D MAKE HIM RUN!

GRRR!

E IS FOR EXTERMINATE ALL SOPPY TOYS.

RAT-TAT-TAT!

F IS FOR FOOD-FIGHT WITH THOSE BASH STREET BOYS.

I IS FOR IVY, THAT'S LITTLE, YOUNG ME.

J IS FOR JAM-JAR, WHERE I KEEP THIS BEE.

BZZZ!

C IS FOR CROCODILE – WATCH WHERE YOU SWIM!

D IS FOR DENNIS – I'M TOUGHER THAN HIM!

G IS FOR GHOST, WISH OUR HOUSE WAS HAUNTED.

H IS FOR HIPPO, THE PET THAT I WANTED.

K IS FOR KILLER, THE CAT FROM NEXT DOOR.

L IS FOR LION THAT GAVE A LOUD ROAR!

M IS FOR MONSTERS WHO THINK THEY ARE SCARY.

N IS FOR NIGHTMARES – ME DRESSED AS A FAIRY!

Q IS FOR QUASIMODO, THE GUY WITH THE HUMP.

R IS FOR ROTTWEILER – I MADE ONE JUMP.

YELP!

U IS FOR UNDERPANTS I FILLED WITH CURRY.

V IS FOR VAMPIRE, WHO LEFT IN A HURRY.

SIZZLE!

BARRY GLENNARD

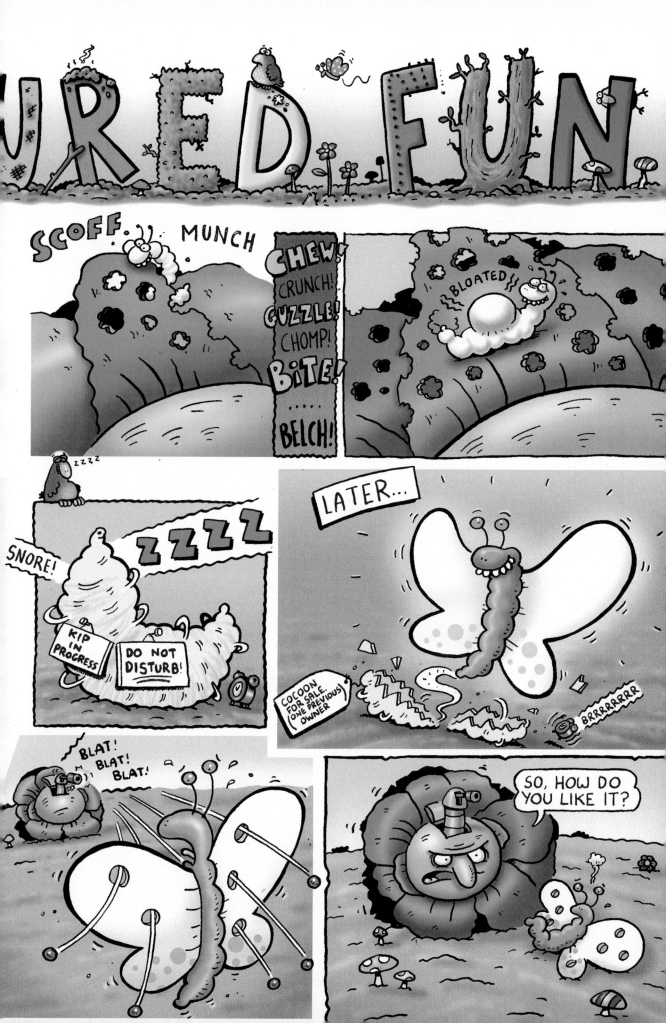

TO FOOTBALLSPEAK

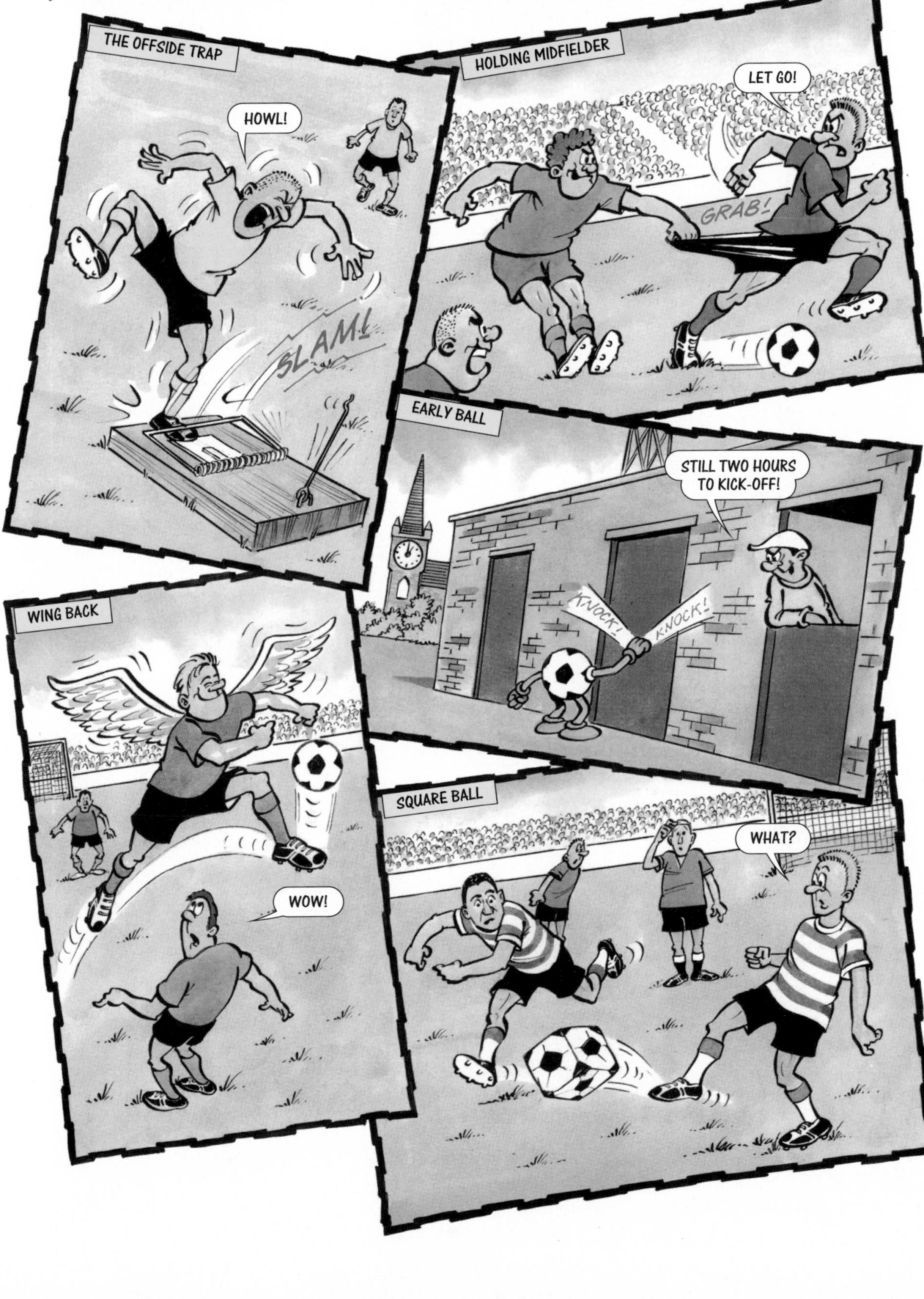

But—

Take a good look at this fairground scene. Once you've done that, turn the page to see the same scene a few minutes later. Pay attention — we'll be asking questions!

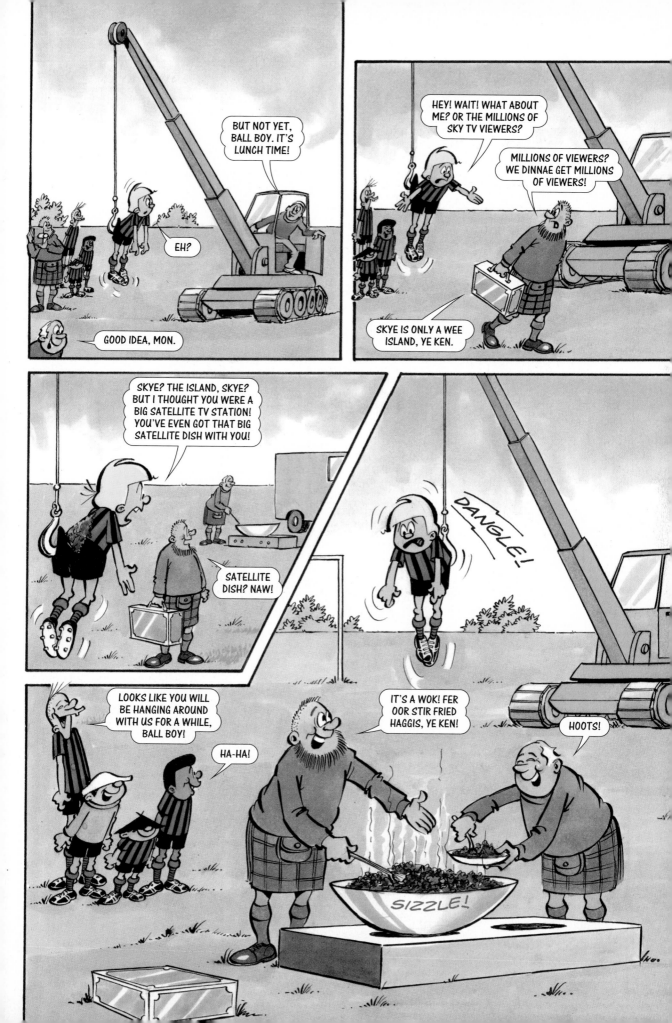

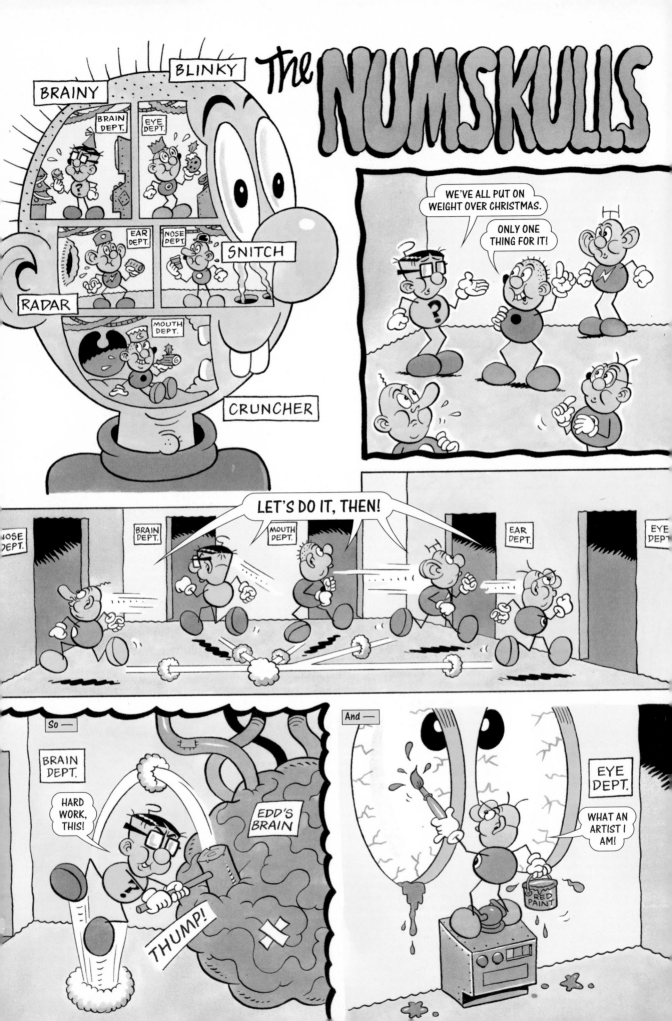

BLUEPRINT : MEN-ACE MACHINES

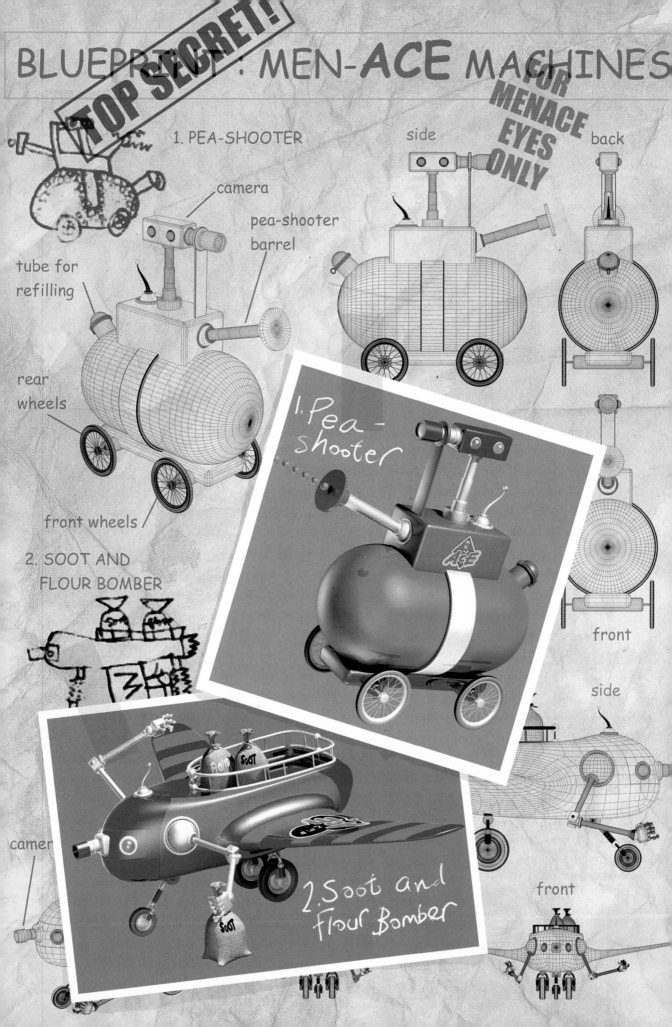

1. PEA-SHOOTER

side

back

camera

pea-shooter barrel

tube for refilling

rear wheels

front wheels

2. SOOT AND FLOUR BOMBER

front

side

1. Pea-shooter

front

side

camera

2. Soot and Flour Bomber

SOOT

FLOUR

SOOT

front

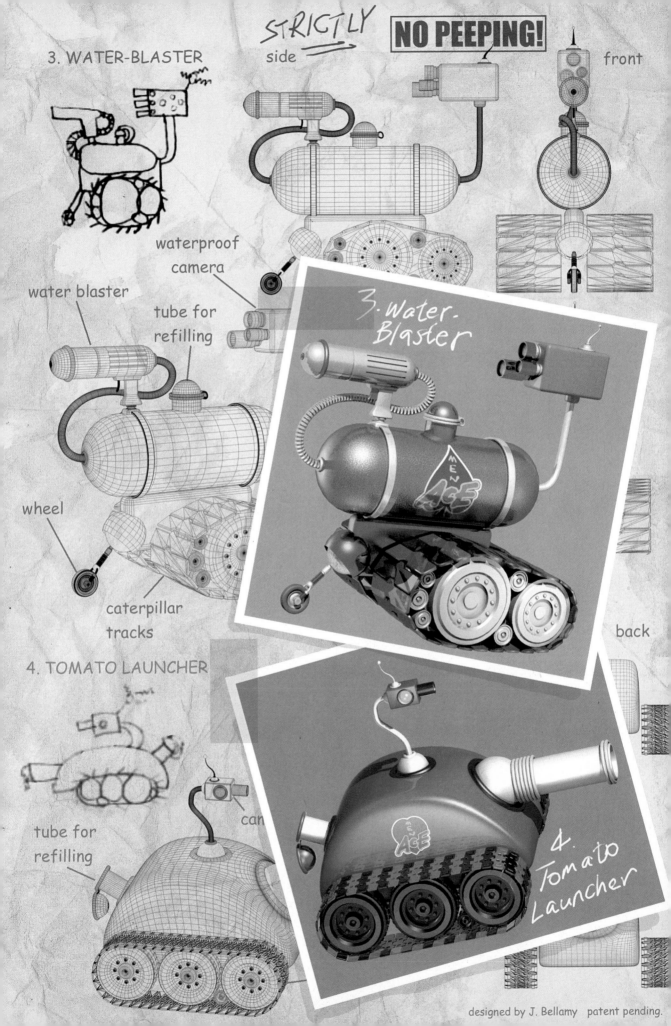

BILLY WHIZZ

THE BASH STREET KIDS in "TEACHER'S PEST!"

ONE DAY, TEACHER WAS GIVING A HISTORY LESSON...

...MMMMMMM...

SNORE!

GLRGRLGGL...

ZZZZZZZZZ...

MAKING BATTLES BORING BY T.D. UMM

Mike Pearse

...AND SO WILLIAM OF NORMANDY... BLAH - BLAH - BLAH ... IN TEN-SIXTY-SIX... ... DRONE - DRONE - DRONE ...

HEY, DANNY! DO YOU WANT A MINT?

OH, THANKS!

SIR! DANNY AND SPOTTY ARE EATING SWEETS IN CLASS!

1

④

AT HOME-TIME...

DRiiING!

ZZZ ... HM?

FREE-DO-O-OM!

TRAMPLE!
TRAMPLE!
TRAMPLE!
TRAMPLE!

CAUGHT OUT AGAIN, CARETAKER?

WHAT A SHAME THOSE KIDS ARE NOT MORE LIKE CUTHBERT.

HM?

WELL, HE'S CLEVER, HE'S HARD-WORKING AND HE'S GOT GOOD MANNERS.

I MEAN, IS THERE ANYTHING THAT BOY HASN'T GOT?

YEAH ...

...FRIENDS.

5

LATER, IN DANNY'S GARDEN SHED....

OKAY, GANG! WE'VE GOT TO DO SOMETHING ABOUT CUTHBERT!

ANY SUGGESTIONS?

IF THIS IS DAFT, SMIFFY, YOU'RE IN FOR A SEVERE SMACKING!

MUNCH! MUNCH! MUNCH!

LET'S SPLATTER HIM WITH WATER BALLOONS!

WE TRIED THAT!

WE TRIED WHAT?

SPLATTERING CUTHBERT WITH WATER BALLOONS!

OH, THAT'S A GOOD ONE! DID EVERYONE HEAR SPOTTY'S IDEA ?!?

GNNNNN...

IDIOT! IDIOT! IDIOT! IDIOT....!

PAF! PAF! PAF! PAF! PAF! PAF!

SIGH! THEY DON'T CALL US 'THE BASH STREET KIDS' FOR NOTHING...

COMPOST

ER ... AM I INTERRUPTING ANYTHING?

6

BONK!

12

AND SO, AT LAST...

Zzz ... HM?

AAAH!

WORRY NOT, DEAR CARETAKER! THOSE RUFFIANS HAVE LEFT AGES AGO!

I STAYED BEHIND TO DO EXTRA WORK.

GIBBER! GIBBER!

YOU SEE, I'VE DECIDED I'M MUCH HAPPIER BEING MYSELF.

SPLASH! SPLOSH! SPLATTER!

GLAD TO HEAR IT, CUTHBERT!

I DO LIKE A HAPPY ENDING, DON'T YOU?

ABSOLUTELY!

SLAP!

THE END

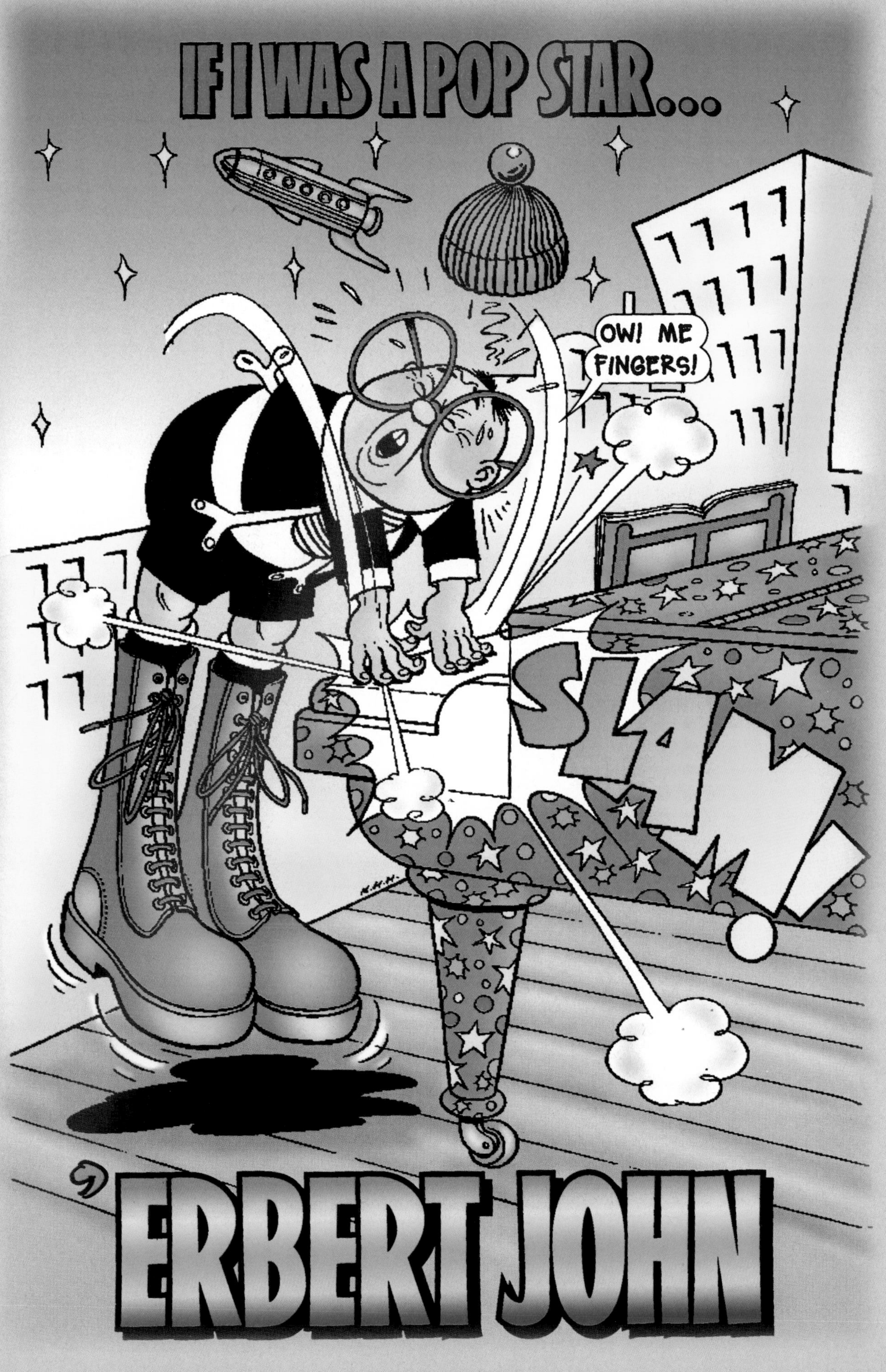
IF I WAS A POP STAR...
OW! ME FINGERS!
SLAM!
'ERBERT JOHN

WOW! COOL!

Tekno Dennis

WAS SENT IN BY LONG-TIME BEANO FAN SIMON
VEGAS FROM ROCHESTER, KENT.

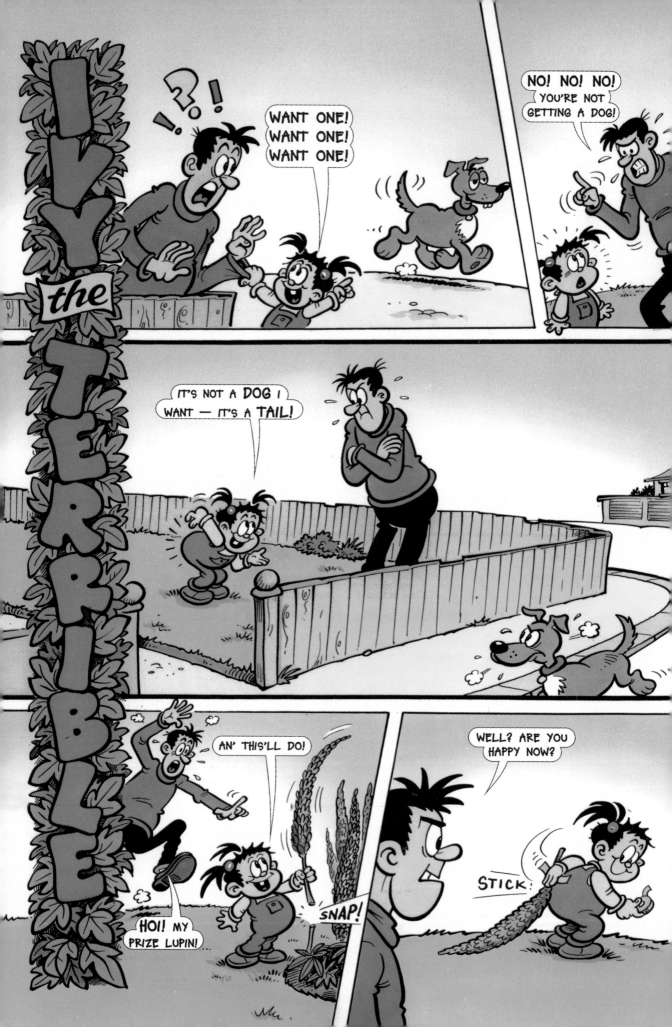

STRIPZ
SPIN!
I LOVE HILL WALKING!
OH-OH! I'M GOING TO SNEEZE!
TEETER!
PECK! PECK! PECK!
MUNCH!
CHOMP!
BLAST!
SHARONS CANNONS Ltd
POP!
THE GREAT BLASTO and Rex

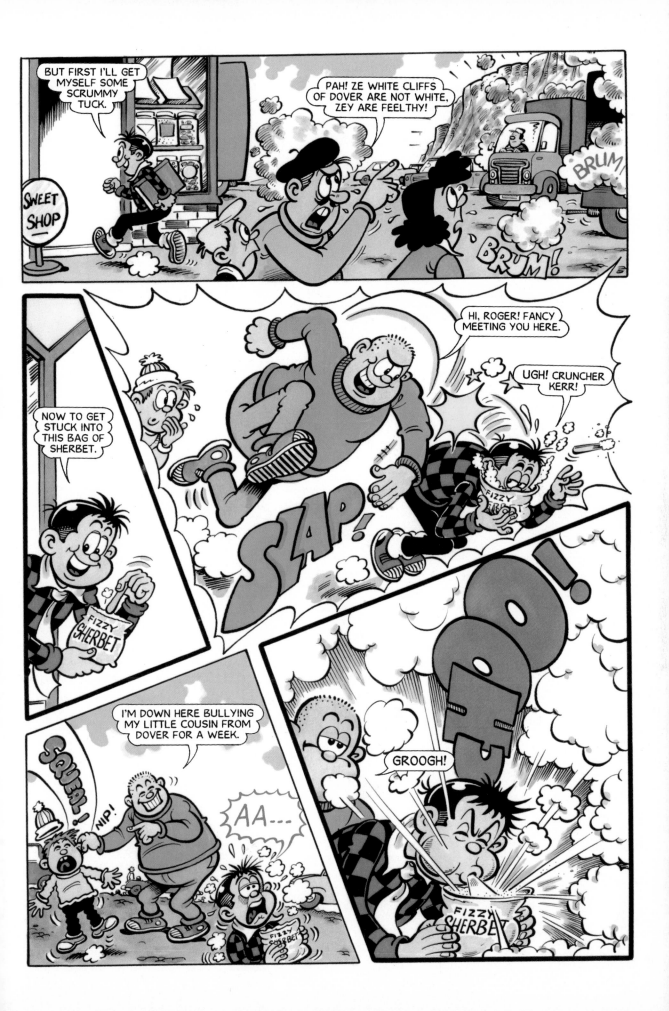

THE COUNTRY
OI! DO YOU MIND?
BRRRM! BRRRM!
I'LL BE GLAD WHEN HE'S OLD ENOUGH FOR A REAL MOTORBIKE.
ER... MAUDE, MAYBE THE STOLE ISN'T SUCH A GOOD IDEA.

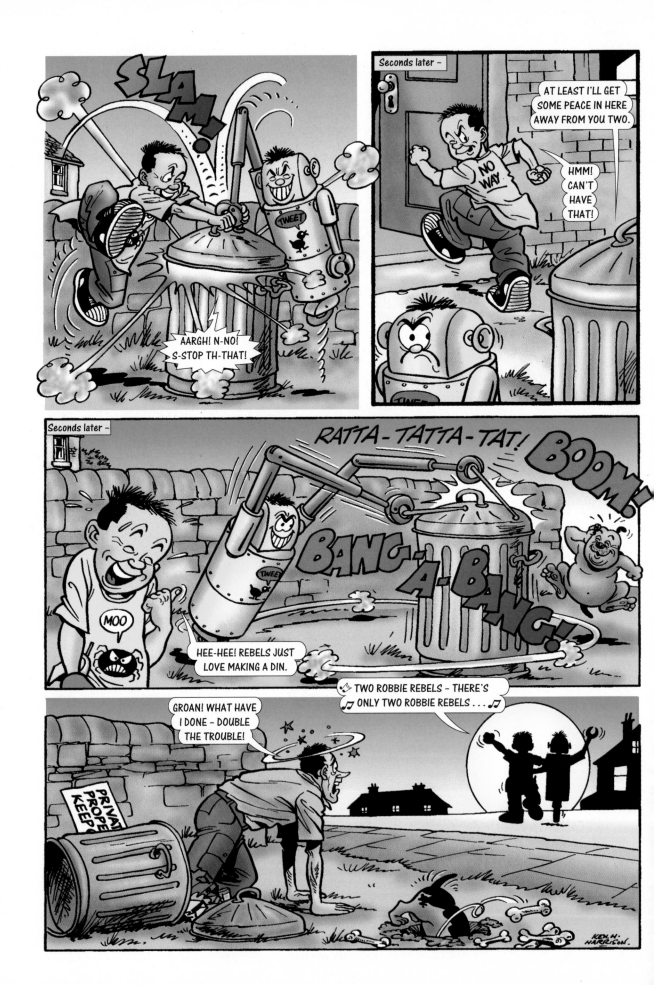

IF WE WERE POP STARS...
JANITOR
GIMME BACK MY MOP TOPS!
THE BASHLES

Poets' Corner

Teacher's version of The Lake Isle of Innisfree by W. B. Yeats.

I shall arise and go now, and go without much glee,
To a small schoolhouse build there of bricks, and plaster made;
Nine wild kids will I teach there, each one out to damage me,
Eight boys and one extreme-loud maid.
And I shall get no peace there, just paint bombs dropping slow,
Dropping from the planes in the rafters as they pull on some strings;
My head will be all splattered, my nose a purple glow,
My jacket like a parrot's wings.
I should arise and go now, but there can be no way,
I hear loo water lapping, then it burst through the door;
While I stand on my desktop, the pupils laugh, and say
'At least your life is not a bore.'

THE LAKE ISLE OF INNISFREE
W. B. Yeats (1865–1939)

I will arise and go now, and go to Innisfree,
And a small cabin build there, of clay and wattles made;
Nine bean rows will I have there, a hive for the honey bee,
And live alone in the bee-loud glade.

And I shall have some peace there, for peace comes dropping slow,
Dropping from the veils of the morning to where the cricket sings;

There midnight's all a-glimmer, and noon a purple glow,
And evening full of the linnet's wings.

I will arise and go now, for always night and day
I hear lake water lapping with low sounds by the shore;
While I stand on the roadway, or on the pavements gray,
I hear it in the deep heart's core.

TO A MOUSE, ON TURNING UP HER NEST WITH THE PLOUGH, NOVEMBER, 1785 Robert Burns (1759–1796)

Wee, sleeket, cowrin, tim'rous beastie,
Oh, what a panic's in thy breastie!
Thou need na start awa sae hasty
Wi' bickerin brattle!
I wad be laith to rin an' chase thee
Wi' murd'ring pattle!

Dennis's version of To A Mouse!
by Robert Burns.

Wee, sleekit, cowrin' tim'rous Wattie,
We' yer saft chummies, Bert and
Spotty.
Just see them start awa sae hasty
Wi' bickerin brattle!
I'll get my sister Bea tae chase thee
Wi' her wee rattle!

Gnasher's version of
Sea Fever by John Masefield.

I must go down to the tree again, to
the lonely tree out by.
And all I ask is a quick wizz
Beneath a star-filled sky.
And the leg lifts and the warm
flow and the small tail wagging,
And a big grin on the dog's face —
never mind Dad's nagging!

SEA FEVER
By John Masefield

I must go down to the seas again, to the lonely sea and the sky, And all I ask is a tall ship and a star to steer her by, And the wheel's kick and the wind's song and the white sail's shaking, And a gray mist on the sea's face, and a gray dawn breaking.

Pie-face's version of
Leisure By W.H. Davies.

What is this pie so full of meat,
I waste no time its crust to eat?
The gravy spurts on Myrtle's blouse
As I scoff chunks of sheep or cows;
No time for beans they give me gas,
I just want pies, you silly ass;
No time for cakes,
though they're all right,
Just feed me pies —
ah, what a sight!

No time to sing,
no time to dance.
I spy a pie — it's got no chance!
No time to wait when my mouth can
Close round a pie — I'm SUCH a fan!
I eat them round, I eat them square.
Aw, they're all done — that's just not fair!

LEISURE W. H. Davies
(1871 — 1940)

What is this life if, full of care,
We have no time to stand and stare?
No time to stand beneath the boughs
And stare as long as sheep or cows;
No time to see, when woods we pass,
Where squirrels hide their nuts in grass;
No time to see, in broad daylight,

Streams full of stars, like skies at night;
No time to turn at Beauty's glance,
And watch her feet, how they can dance;
No time to wait till her mouth can
Enrich that smile her eyes began?
A poor life this if, full of care,
We have no time to stand and stare.

IF WE WERE POP STARS...
GNOASIS
TOP OF THE POPS
WOW! HANDSOME EYEBROWS!
GB
B
F
F
KHN.

Gemma Asterling,
Grimsby

India Custance, Farnham, Surrey

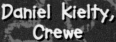

Daniel Kielty,
Crewe

William
Challands,
Sheffield